I0415082

This Book Belongs To:

BY
Home Planners And Journals

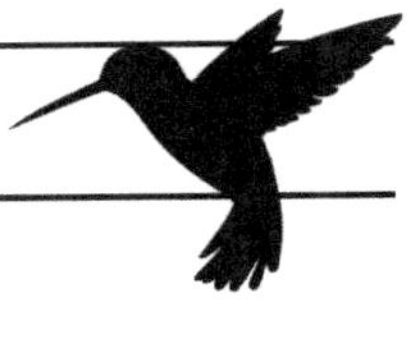

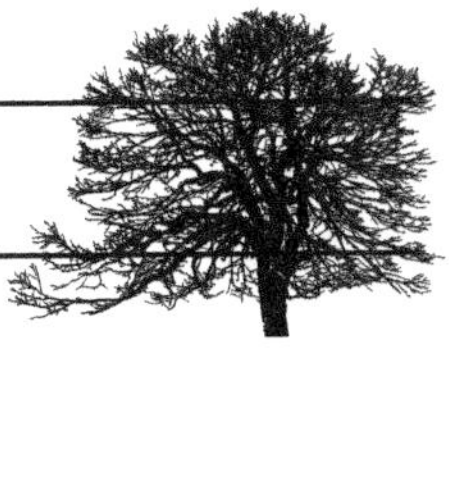

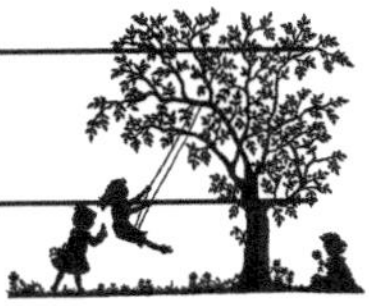

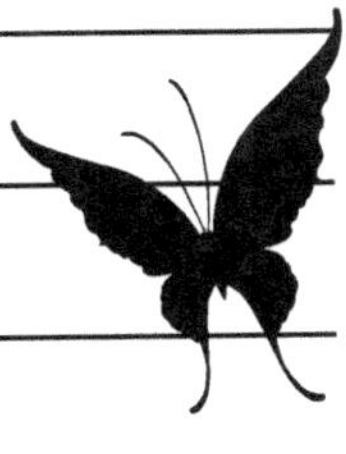

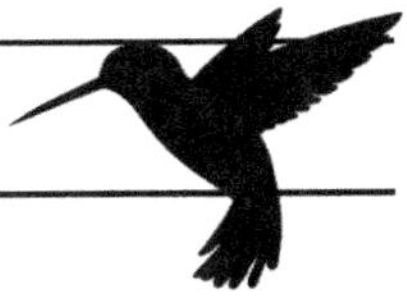

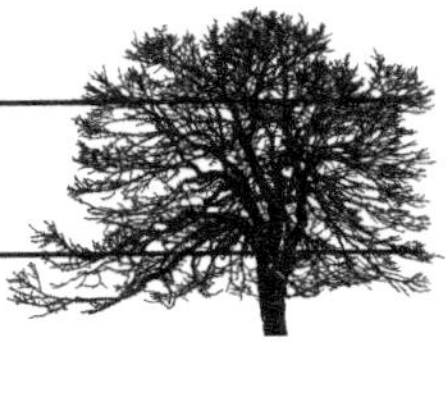

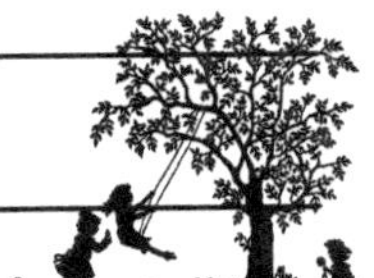

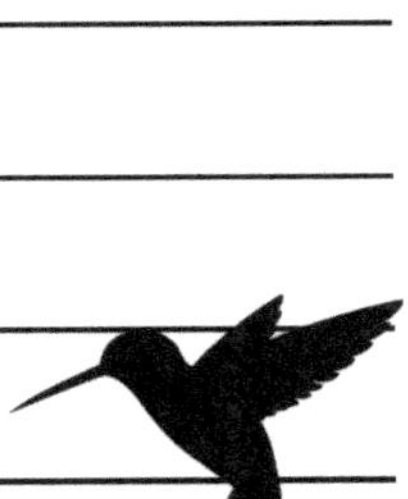

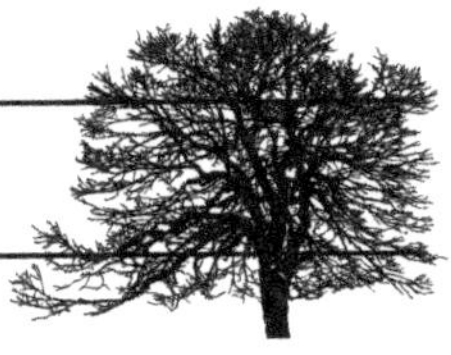

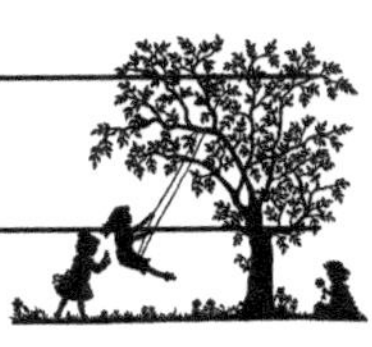

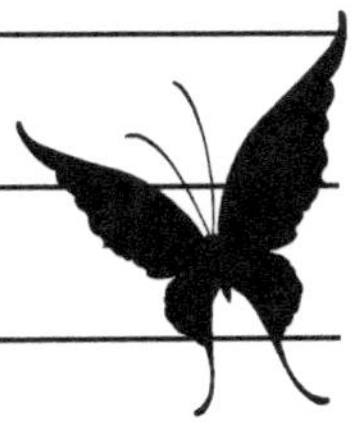

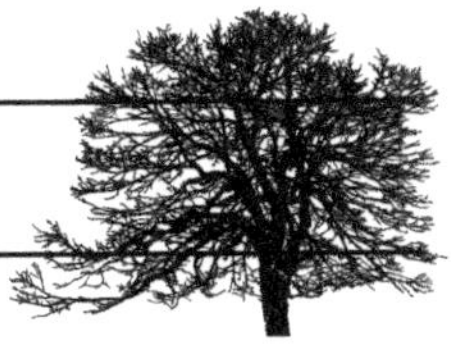

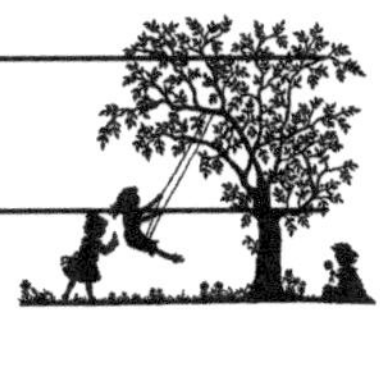

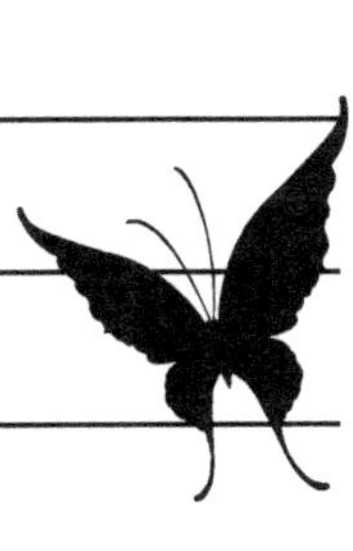

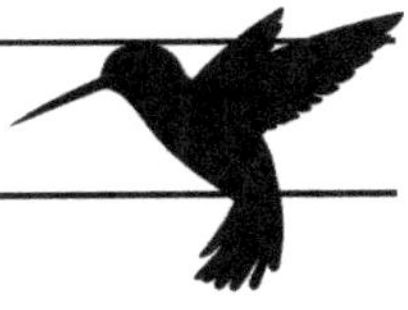

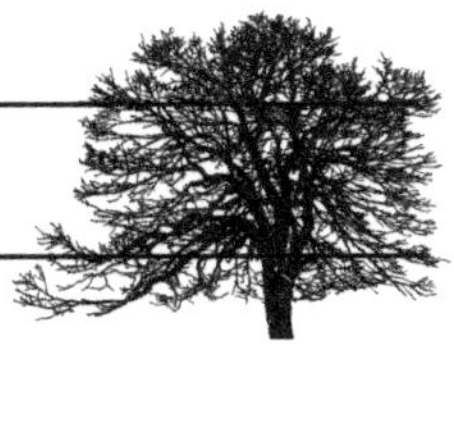

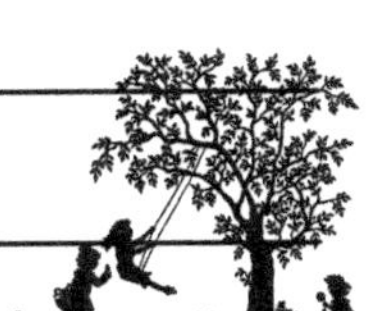

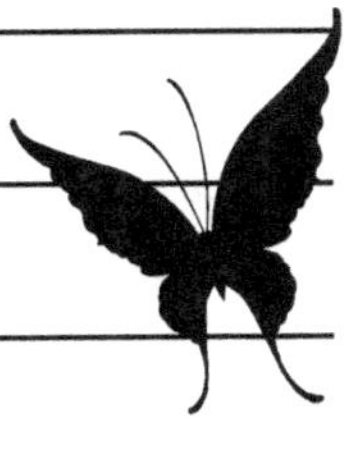

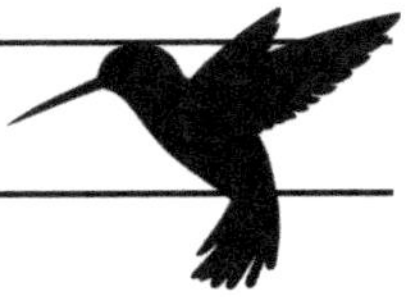

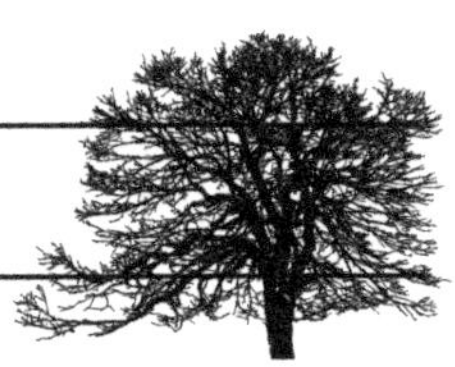

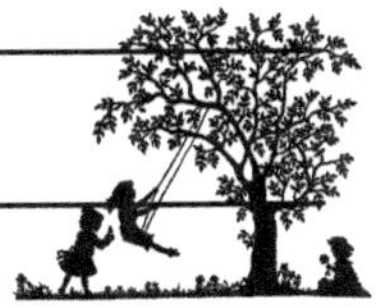

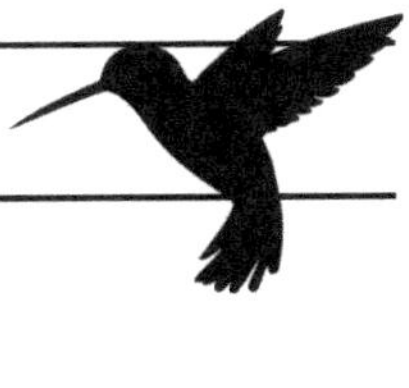

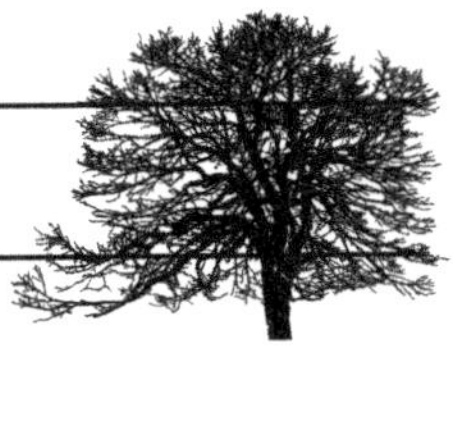

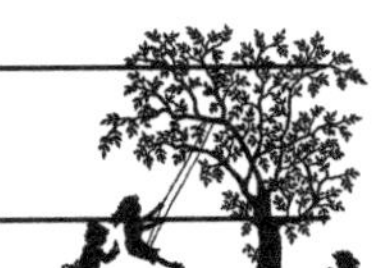

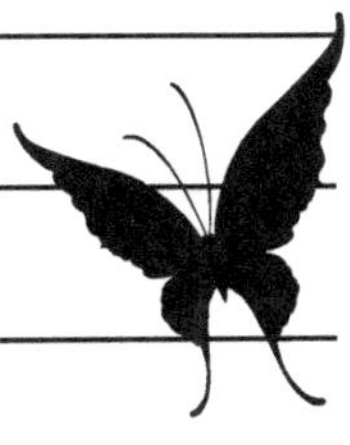

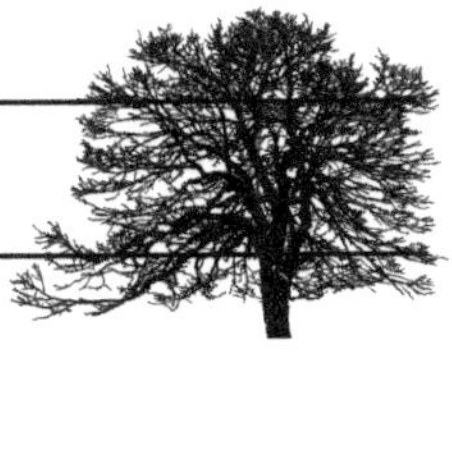

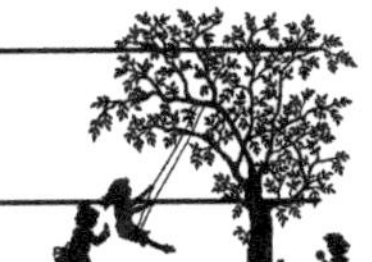

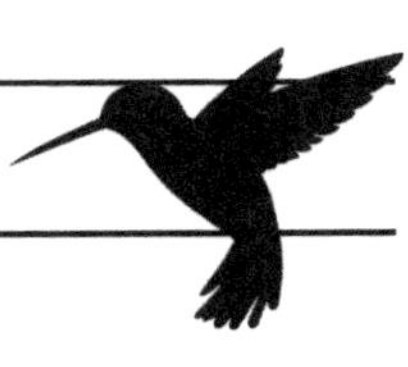

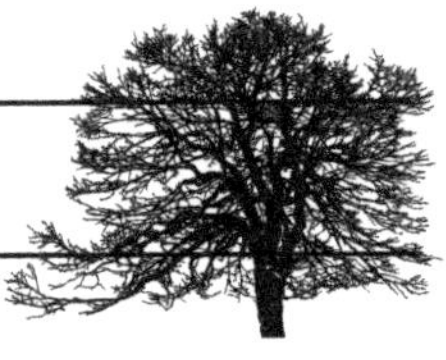

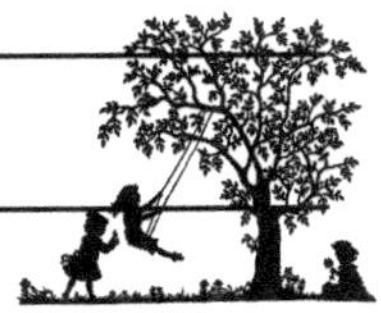

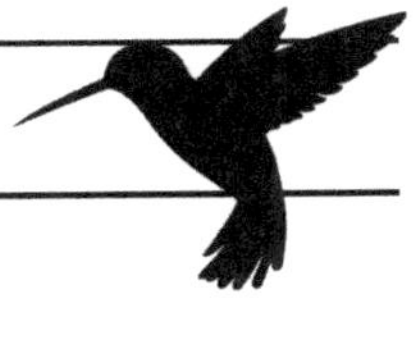

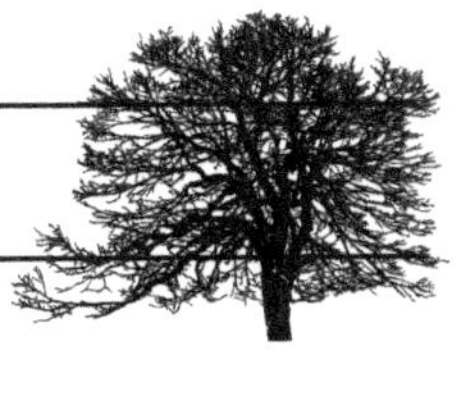

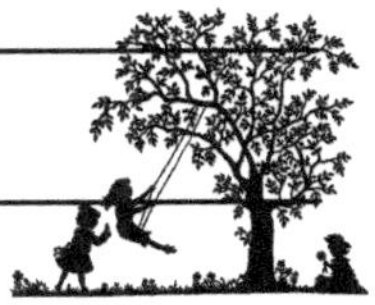

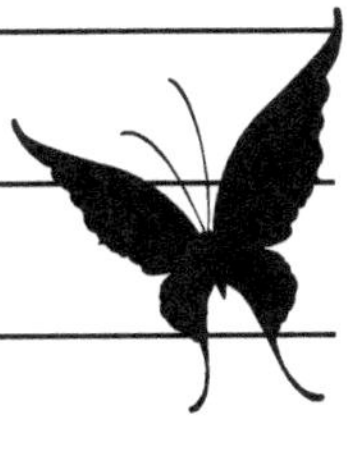

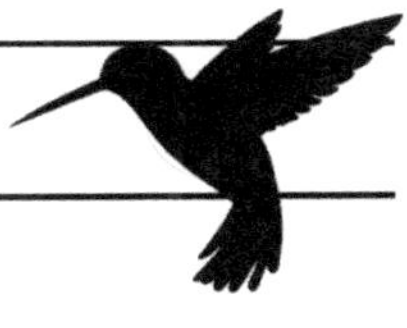

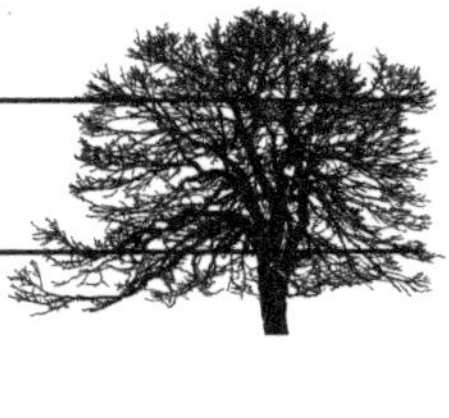

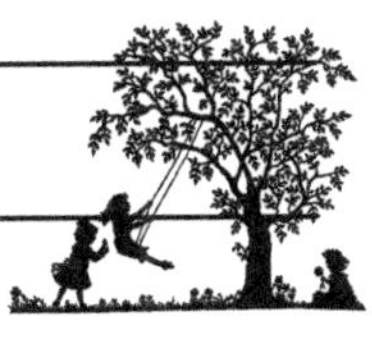

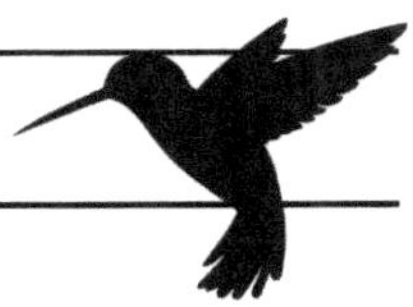

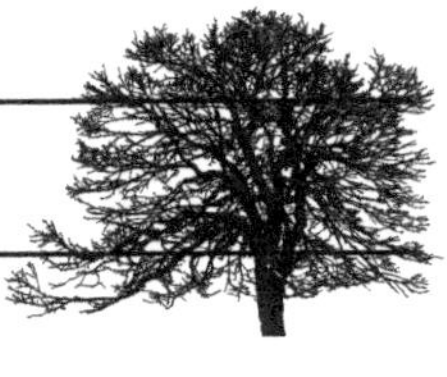

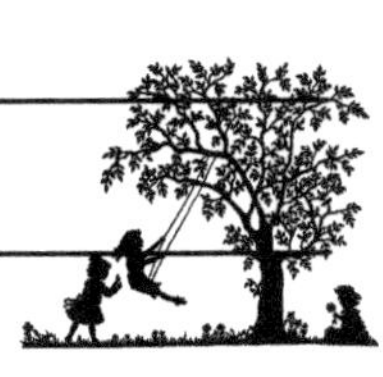

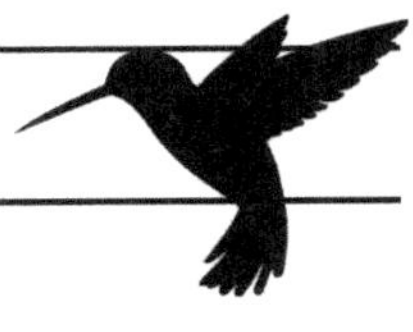

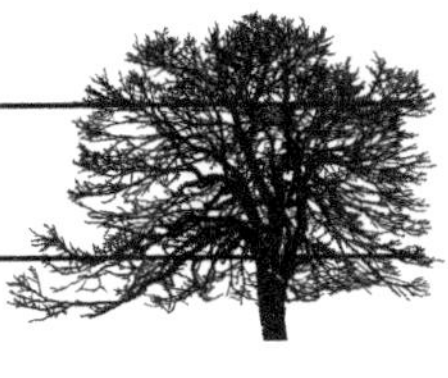

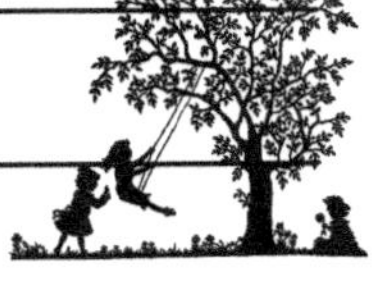

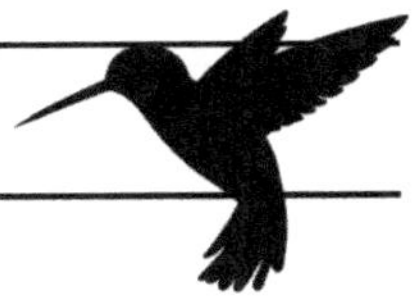

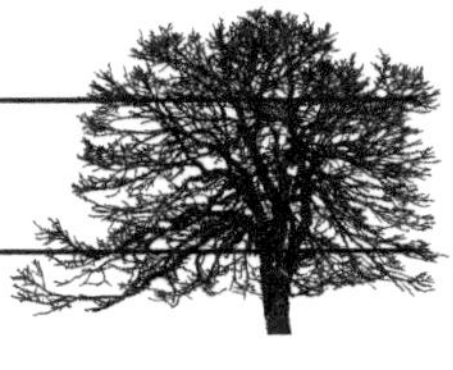

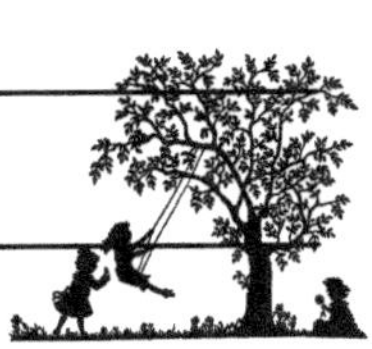

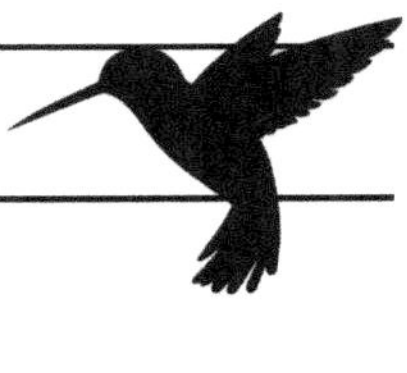

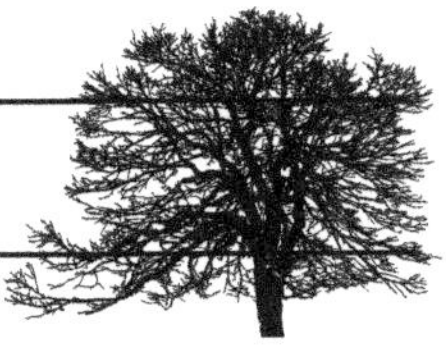

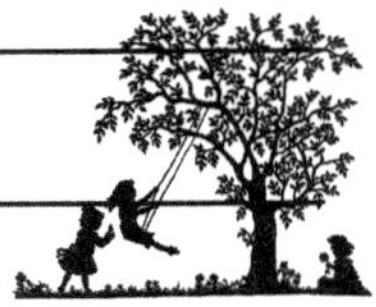

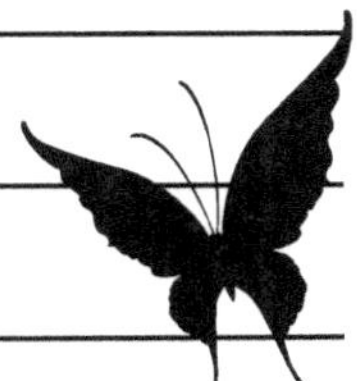

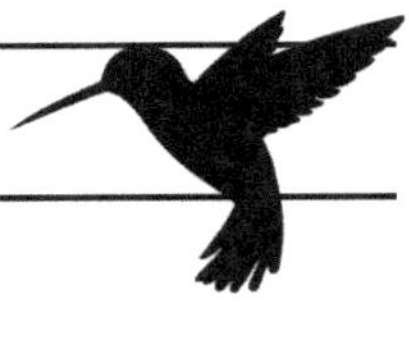

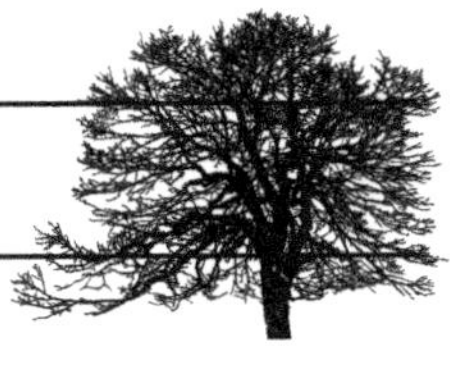

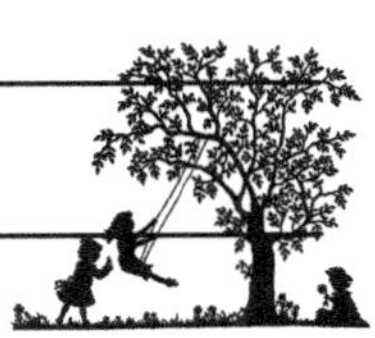

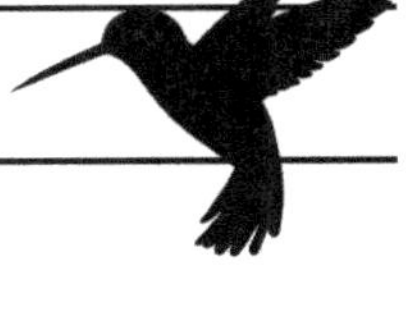

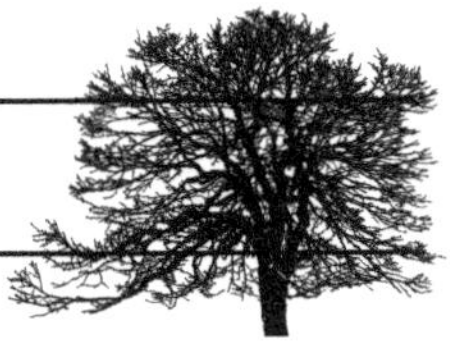

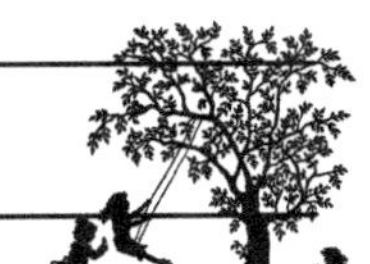

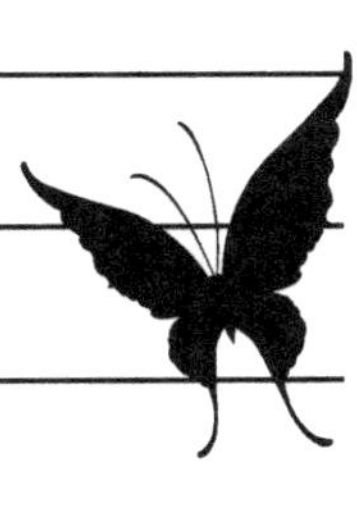

www.ingramcontent.com/pod-product-compliance
Lightning Source LLC
Chambersburg PA
CBHW072051280526
45788CB00006B/2261
* 9 7 8 1 0 9 0 2 3 3 7 6 9 *